MW00388541

Writing Prompts from Grimm:

A Fairy-tale Themed Workbook for Grades 7-12

Shonna Slayton

AMARETTO PRESS

Copyright © 2020 by Shonna Slayton

All rights reserved. No portion of this book may be reproduced in any form without permission from the publisher, except as permitted by U.S. copyright law.

For permissions use the contact form on
www.ShonnaSlayton.com

Cover and interior art by Seedlings Design Studio
Interior by SaRose Design

ISBN: 978-1-947736-02-3

Amaretto Press
Phoenix, AZ

Other Books by Shonna Slayton

Nonfiction

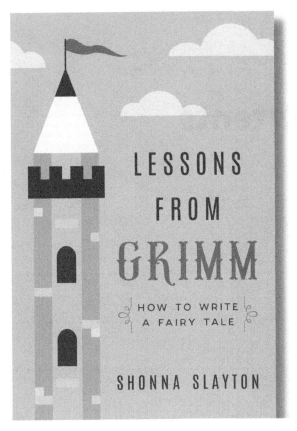

Lessons From Grimm: How To Write a Fairy Tale
Lessons From Grimm: How to Write a Fairy Tale (workbook series)
Writing Prompts From Grimm: A fairy-tale themed workbook for Grades 3-6

Fiction

Fairy-tale Inheritance Series

Cinderella's Dress
Cinderella's Shoes
Cinderella's Legacy
Snow White's Mirror
Beauty's Rose

Lost Fairy Tales Series

The Tower Princess

Writing Prompts from Grimm

A fairy-tale themed workbook for Grades 7-12

Table of Contents

Note to Students: In this book you'll get to work with beginning, middle, and ending prompts quoted from Grimms' fairy tales. You can write the story directly onto the page or use the space for brainstorming.

Beginnings: In these prompts, the Grimms start the story for you, giving you characters and setting. You get to come up with the conflict and the plot. Start by thinking about what could go wrong…

Middles: Here you are stuck in the middle. What happened before? And what is going to happen after? Remember to introduce your characters and show us the setting where the story is taking place.

Endings: Work backward to find out how the characters ended up here. It's like you are a fairy tale detective and have to piece all the evidence together.

Appendix: Look here to find out which story the prompt came from. Then go and compare your story with the Grimms' original.

Note to educators: Each section works on a different aspect of storytelling and logical thinking. Think of the formula as ABC.

In the **beginning prompts**, students are given "A" and have to come up with what leads to "B" and "C." Generally, these prompts give characters and setting, but few clues about conflict and plot. Middle prompts work on the middle logic of a story. Students are given "B" and have to come up with a logical start "A" as well as a logical conclusion, "C." Students might find these the most challenging.

Endings: Starting with the conclusion, "C," students work the logic backward to arrive at "A" and "B." They have to come up with characters and motivations and a logical plot that makes sense with the ending.

Note regarding Grimm: The prompts have been slightly modified from Margaret Hunt's 1884 translation, using some updated language for today's reader. Be aware that Grimms' version of the fairy tales are the ones where toes are cut off to fit into shoes (Cinderella) or "heads roll" when the merchant's son becomes king of the Golden Mountain. Consider previewing the stories so you're not surprised.

1.   <u>Title :</u> _____

In old times when wishing still helped, there lived a king whose daughters were all beautiful, but the youngest was so beautiful that the sun itself, which has seen so much, was astonished whenever it shone in her face.

2.   Title: _____

Near a great forest dwelt a wood-cutter with his wife, who had an only child, a little girl three years old.

3.   Title: _____

There was once an old king who was ill, and thought to himself, "I am lying on what must be my death-bed."

4.   <u>Title:</u> _____

There were once a king and a queen who lived happily together and had twelve children, but they were all boys.

5.   Title: _____

A long time ago there lived a king who was famed for his wisdom through all the land.

6.   <u>Title:</u> _____

One summer's morning a little tailor was sitting on his table by the window; he was in good spirits, and sewed with all his might.

7.   Title:_____

There was once a King's son who was seized with a desire to travel about the world, and took no one with him but a faithful servant.

8. <u>Title:</u> _____

A certain miller had little by little fallen into poverty, and had nothing left but his mill and a large apple tree behind it.

9.   Title: _____

A certain mother's child had been taken away out of its cradle by the elves, and a changeling with a large head and staring eyes, which would do nothing but eat and drink, laid in its place.

10. Title: _____

In the olden time there was a king, who had behind his palace a beautiful pleasure-garden in which there was a tree that bore golden apples. When the apples were getting ripe they were counted, but on the very next morning one was missing.

11. Title: _____

There were once upon a time two brothers, one rich and the other poor. The rich one was a goldsmith and evil-hearted.

12. Title: _____

There was once an old castle in the midst of a large and thick forest, and in it an old woman who was a witch dwelt all alone.

13. Title: _____

A father once called his three sons before him, and he gave to the first a rooster, to the second a scythe, and to the third a cat.

14. Title: _____

There was once a man who was about to set out on a long journey, and on parting he asked his three daughters what he should bring back for them.

15. Title: _____

There was once upon a time a rich King who had three daughters, who daily went to walk in the palace garden, and the King was a great lover of all kinds of fine trees, but there was one for which he had such an affection, that if anyone gathered an apple from it he wished him a hundred fathoms underground.

16. <u>Title:</u> _____

About a thousand or more years ago, there were in this country nothing but small kings, and one of them who lived on the Keuterberg was very fond of hunting.

17. Title: _____

There was once a King who had an illness, and no one believed that he would come out of it with his life.

18. Title: _____

There was once a young fellow who had learnt the trade of locksmith, and told his father he would now go out into the world and seek his fortune.

19.   Title: _____

In the days when wishing was still of some use, a King's son was bewitched by an old witch, and shut up in an iron stove in a forest.

20. Title: _____

There was once a poor man who had four sons, and when they were grown up, he said to them, "My dear children, you must now go out into the world, for I have nothing to give you, so set out, and go to some distance and learn a trade, and see how you can make your way."

21. Title: _____

There was once a King who had a great forest near his palace, full of all kinds of wild animals.

22. Title: _____

There was once a poor widow who lived in a lonely cottage. In front of the cottage was a garden wherein stood two rose-trees, one of which bore white and the other red roses.

23. Title: _____

Twelve servants who had done nothing all the day would not exert themselves at night either, but laid themselves on the grass and boasted of their idleness.

24. <u>Title:</u> _____

There was once upon a time a very old woman, who lived with the flock of geese in a waste place among the mountains, and there had a little house.

25. Title: _____

There was once upon a time a princess, who, high under the battlements in her castle, had an apartment with twelve windows, which looked out in every possible direction, and when she climbed up to it and looked around her, she could inspect her whole kingdom.

26. Title: _____

A young drummer went out quite alone one evening into the country, and came to a lake on the shore of which he perceived three pieces of white linen lying.

27. Title: _____

There was once a King who had a daughter, and he ordered a glass mountain to be made, and said that whosoever could cross to the other side of it without falling should have his daughter to wife.

28. Title: _____

There was once an enchantress, who had three sons who loved each other as brothers, but the old woman did not trust them, and thought they wanted to steal her power from her.

29.   Title: _____

A shoemaker, by no fault of his own, had become so poor that at last he had nothing left but leather for one pair of shoes.

30. Title: _____

Two or three hundred years ago, when people were far from being so crafty and cunning as they are now-a-day, an extraordinary event took place in a little town.

31. Title: _____

The fishes had for a long time been discontented because no order prevailed in their kingdom.

32. Title: _____

There was once a forester who went into the forest to hunt, and as he entered it he heard a sound of screaming as if a little child were there.

33. Title: _____

There was once upon a time a tailor who had three sons and only one goat.

34. Title: _____

There was once a King who had a little boy of whom it had been foretold that he should be killed by a stag when he was sixteen years of age, and when he had reached that age the huntsmen went hunting with him.

1.   Title:_____

He held in his hand a black spear and said, "I give you this spear because your heart is pure and good; with this you can boldly attack the wild boar, and it will do you no harm."

2.   Title:_____

The King's daughter was now a kitchen-maid, and had to be at the cook's beck and call, and do the dirtiest work.

3. Title: _____

But suddenly he came into her room, and said, "Now give me what you promised."

4. Title: _____

At length the three brothers arrived at a castle where stone horses were standing in the stables, and no human being was to be seen, and they went through all the halls until, quite at the end, they came to a door in which were three locks.

5.   Title: _____

He sat down and was sad, then all at once he saw that there was a trap-door close by the feather. He raised it up, found some steps, and went down them, and then he came to another door, knocked at it, and heard somebody inside calling.

6.   Title: _____

Now the host had three daughters, who saw the goose and were curious to know what such a wonderful bird might be, and would have liked to have one of its golden feathers.

7.   Title: _____

It happened, however, that one day a feast was held in the palace, and she said to the cook, "May I go upstairs for a while and look on? I will place myself outside the door."

8.   Title: _____

Then came the old cook, who knew that the child had the power of wishing, and stole it away, and he took a hen, and cut it in pieces, and dropped some of its blood on the Queen's apron and on her dress.

9.   <u>Title:</u> _____

When he was asleep, she first drew the ring from his finger, then she drew away the foot which was under him, leaving only the slipper behind her, and she took her child in her arms, and wished herself back in her own kingdom.

10. Title: _____

It stood on a glass-mountain, and the bewitched maiden drove in her carriage round the castle, and then went inside it.

11. Title: _____

Then she ordered a powerful sleeping draught to be brought, to drink farewell to him; the King took a long draught, but she took only a little.

12. Title: _____

So she took him with her into her enchanted castle, where there were nothing but cats who were her servants.

13. Title: _____

Now it came to pass that another King came journeying by with his attendants and runners, and he also had lost his way, and did not know how to get home again because the forest was so large.

14. <u>Title:</u>_____

They all three announced themselves to the princess, and said she was to propound her riddle to them, and that the right persons were now come, who had understandings so fine that they could be threaded in a needle.

15. Title: _____

The dream may have been true," said the King, "I will give you a piece of advice. Fill your pocket full of peas, and make a small hole in it, and then if you are carried away again, they will fall out and leave a track in the streets."

16. <u>Title:</u> _____

With that he picked himself out a fine head of cabbage, and ate it, but scarcely had he swallowed a couple of mouthfuls than he felt very strange and quite different.

17. Title: _____

When, however, she had sat there for a while, a white dove came flying to her with a little golden key in its mouth.

18. Title: _____

Next morning, when they all awoke, and went to the door, there stood a strangely magnificent tree with leaves of silver, and fruit of gold hanging among them, so that in all the wide world there was nothing more beautiful or precious.

19. Title:_____

When they were all ready they looked carefully at the soldier, but he had closed his eyes and did not move or stir, so they felt themselves quite secure.

20. Title: _____

Whilst he was standing there undecided, a voice sounded out of the rock, which cried to him, "Enter without fear; no evil shall befall you."

21. Title: _____

As he spoke so pleasantly, the door-keeper thought he could not be telling a lie, and asked him to go in, and he was right, for when Hans uncovered his basket in the King's presence, golden-yellow apples came tumbling out.

22. Title: _____

At last she hired herself to a farmer as a cow-herd, and buried her dresses and jewels beneath a stone.

23. Title: _____

Her father's castle lay in ruins, the town and the villages were, so far as could be seen, destroyed by fire, the fields far and wide laid to waste, and no human being was visible.

24. Title: _____

Then the dragon rushed upon the huntsman, but he swung his sword until it sang through the air, and struck off three of his heads.

25. <u>Title:</u> _____

Now it so happened that on this very day the Queen lost her most beautiful ring, and suspicion of having stolen it fell upon this trusty servant, who was allowed to go everywhere.

26. Title: _____

He took a ring from his finger, broke it in two, and gave her one half, the other he kept for himself.

27. Title: _____

While she sat so contentedly there thinking of no ill luck, the cat came creeping in, found the cup-board open, took the hand and heart and eyes of the three army-surgeons, and ran off with them.

28. Title: _____

He soon saw that she was the Nix of the Mill-pond, and in his fright did not know whether he should run away or stay where he was.

29. Title: _____

The giant was so terribly alarmed that he could not close an eye all night long for thinking what would be the best way to get rid of this accursed sorcerer of a servant.

30. Title: _____

He took the basket to the judge, but when the judge had read the letter, and counted the bunches he said, "Two clusters are wanting."

31. Title: _____

Then she was much troubled, and went to her father and mother and asked if it was true that she had had brothers, and what had become of them?

32. <u>Title:</u>_____

He crept like a snail to a well in a field, and there he thought that he would rest and refresh himself with a cool draught of water, but in order that he might not injure the stones in sitting down, he laid them carefully by his side on the edge of the well.

33. Title:_____

Only you must take care to make my bed well, and shake it thoroughly till the feathers fly for then there is snow on the earth.

1. Title: _____

And as soon as she was burnt the roebuck changed his shape, and received his human form again, so the sister and brother lived happily together all their lives.

2.　Title: _____

"You have pronounced your own sentence;" and he ordered such a barrel to be brought, and the old woman to be put into it with her daughter, and then the top was hammered on, and the barrel rolled down hill until it went into the river.

Writing Prompts from Grimm

3.   Title: _____

And thus she got rid of the hateful flax-spinning.

4.   Title:_____

Then she was placed with her accomplice in a ship which had been pierced with holes, and sent out to sea, where they soon sank amid the waves.

Writing Prompts from Grimm

5.   Title: _____

"Go to her, and you will find her back again in the dirty hovel." And there they are living still at this very time.

6.   <u>Title:</u>_____

But the King and the Queen with their six brothers lived many years in happiness and peace.

7. Title: _____

Thereupon the wedding was celebrated, and the lion was again taken into favor, because, after all, he had told the truth.

8.   Title:_____

Then the six conveyed the riches home, divided it amongst them, and lived in content until their death.

9.   Title: _____

And when the sentence had been carried out, the young King married his true bride, and both of them reigned over their kingdom in peace and happiness.

10. <u>Title:</u>_____

And when he had done that, the white horse stood up on its hind legs, and was changed into a King's son.

11. Title: _____

The spindle, shuttle, and needle were preserved in the treasure-chamber, and held in great honor.

12.   Title: _____

And the ungrateful son was forced to feed the toad every day, or else it fed itself on his face; and thus he went about the world without knowing rest.

13. <u>Title:</u> _____

When the seven kids saw that, they came running to the spot and cried aloud, "The wolf is dead! The wolf is dead!" and danced for joy round about the well with their mother.

14. <u>Title:</u> _____

The musician, however, played once more to the man out of gratitude, and then went onwards.

15. Title: _____

Then he made a vow to take no more ragamuffins into his house, for they consume much, pay for nothing, and play mischievous tricks into the bargain by way of gratitude.

16. Title: _____

The bean thanked him most prettily, but as the tailor used black thread, all beans since then have a black seam.

17. Title: _____

Owing to his carelessness the wood caught fire, that a conflagration ensued, the bird hastened to fetch water, and then the bucket dropped from his claws into the well, and he fell down with it, and could not recover himself, but had to drown there.

18.   Title:_____

After this the robbers did not trust themselves in the house again; but it suited the four musicians so well that they did not care to leave it any more.

19. Title: _____

But from this time forth the King had to ferry, as a punishment for his sins. Perhaps he is ferrying still? If he is, it is because no one has taken the oar from him.

20. Title:_____

Then she ran out of the village, and no one has seen her since.

21. Title: _____

They gave him to eat and to drink, and had some new clothes made for him, for his own had been spoiled on his journey.

22. Title: _____

And she had not, as she thought, been three days with the little men in the mountains, but seven years, and in the meantime her former masters had died.

23. Title: _____

The dog and cat looked up and saw the wolf, who was ashamed of having shown himself so timid, and he made friends with the dog.

24. Title:_____

And they hovered about there in the air, and could not get to each other, and whether they are still hovering about, or not, I do not know, but the young giant took up his iron bar, and went on his way.

25. Title: _____

Then Dr. Knowall showed the count where the money was, but did not say who had stolen it, and received from both sides much money in reward, and became a renowned man.

26. Title: _____

At last when only one single house remained, the child came home and just said, "Stop, little pot," and it stopped and gave up cooking, and whosoever wished to return to the town had to eat his way back.

27. <u>Title:</u> _____

He kept his word, but the poor goldsmith was obliged to carry the two humps as long as he lived, and to cover his bald head with a cap.

28. Title:_____

"And that unlucky nail," said he to himself, "has caused all this disaster."

29. Title: _____

There he reduced the dead to subjection, bade them lie down in their graves again, took the moon away with him, and hung it up in heaven.

30. <u>Title:</u> _____

Two of her tears wetted his eyes and they grew clear again, and he could see with them as before. He led her to his kingdom where he was joyfully received, and they lived for a long time afterwards, happy and contented.

Writing Prompts from Grimm

31. Title: _____

And thus, for their wickedness and falsehood, they were punished with blindness as long as they lived.

32. Title:_____

Thereupon he mounted the student's horse and rode away, but in an hour's time sent someone to let the student out again.

33.   <u>Title:</u> _____

On the same morning, the rose was in full bloom.

Appendix: Grimm Prompts Source Key

Beginnings

1. The Frog King, 2. Our Lady's Child (Mary's Child), 3. Faithful John, 4. The Twelve Brothers, 5. The White Snake, 6. The Valiant Little Tailor, 7. The Riddle, 8. The Girl without Hands, 9. The Elves, Third Story, 10. The Golden Bird, 11. The Two Brothers, 12. Jorinda and Joringel, 13. The Three Sons of Fortune, 14. The Singing, Soaring Lark, 15. The Gnome, 16. The Three Little Birds, 17. The Water of Life, 18. The Skillful Huntsman, 19. The Iron Stove, 20. The Four Skillful Brothers, 21. Iron John, 22. Snow-White and Rose-Red, 23. The Twelve Idle Servants, 24. The Goose-Girl at the Well, 25. The Sea-Hare, 26. The Drummer, 27. Old Rinkrank, 28. The Crystal Ball, 29. The Elves and the Shoemaker, 30. The Owl, 31. The Sole, 32. The Foundling, 33. The Wishing-Table, The Gold Donkey, and the Cudgel in the Sack, 34. The Two Kings' Children.

Middles

1. The Singing Bone, 2. King Thrushbeard, 3. Rumpelstiltskin, 4. The Queen Bee, 5. The Three Feathers, 6. The Golden Goose, 7. Allerleirauh (All Kinds of Fur), 8. The Pink, 9. The King of the Golden Mountain, 10. The Raven, 11. The Peasant's Wise Daughter, 12. The Poor Miller's Boy and the Cat, 13. Hans the Hedgehog, 14. The Cunning Little Tailor, 15. The Blue Light, 16. Donkey Cabbages, 17. The Old Woman in the Wood, 18. One-Eye, Two-Eyes, and Three-Eyes, 19. The Shoes that Were Danced to Pieces, 20. The Glass Coffin, 21. The Griffin, 22. The True Sweethearts (The True Bride), 23. Maid Maleen, 24. The Two Brothers, 25. The White Snake, 26. Bearskin, 27. The Three Army Surgeons, 28. The Nix of the Mill-Pond, 29. The Giant and the Tailor, 30. The Poor Boy in the Grave, 31. The Seven Ravens, 32. Hans in Luck, 33. Mother Holle

Endings

1. Brother and Sister, 2. The Three Little Men in the Wood, 3. The Three Spinning Women, 4. The Three Snake-Leaves, 5. The Fisherman and his Wife, 6. The Six Swans, 7. The Twelve Huntsmen, 8. How Six Men Got On in the World, 9. The Goose-Girl, 10. Ferdinand the Faithful, 11. The Spindle, The Shuttle, and The Needle, 12. The Ungrateful Son, 13. The Wolf and the Seven Little Kids, 14. The Wonderful Musician, 15. The Pack of Ragamuffins, 16. The Straw, the Coal, and the Bean, 17. The Mouse, the Bird, and the Sausage, 18. The Bremen Town-Musicians, 19. The Devil with the Three Golden Hairs, 20. Clever Elsie, 21. Thumbling, 22. The Elves, Second Story, 23. Old Sultan, 24. The Young Giant, 25. Doctor Knowall, 26. Sweet Porridge, 27. The Little Folks' Presents, 28. The Nail, 29. The Moon, 30. Rapunzel, 31. Cinderella, 32. The Turnip, 33. The Rose.

Made in the USA
Monee, IL
22 July 2020

36845315R00059